Chuckwagon
RACING

Rob Waring, *Series Editor*

HEINLE
CENGAGE Learning™

Australia • Brazil • Japan • Korea • Mexico • Singapore • Spain • United Kingdom • United States

Words to Know

This story is set in Canada, in the city of Calgary [kælgəri]. The city is in the province of Alberta [ælbɜrtə], which is in the western part of the country.

A **A Cowboy's Life.** Read the paragraph. Then match each word with the correct definition.

Long ago, cowboys lived a special life. They slept in tents and cooked their food on a small stove. They usually kept their food and equipment in a chuckwagon to make it easy to relocate. These cowboys were very skilled at working with horses and cattle. Nowadays, cowboys—and cowgirls—often compete in rodeos to test their own cowboy skills. These events are very popular in parts of the U.S. and Canada.

1. tent _____

2. stove _____

3. chuckwagon _____

4. cattle _____

5. rodeo _____

a. a moveable covering in which to sleep

b. a piece of equipment used to cook food

c. an old-style vehicle with four wheels that carries equipment and food

d. an event that tests cowboy skills

e. a group of large animals which are raised for milk, food, and leather

cattle

Cowboys Camping

B At the Rodeo.

Write each word in this picture next to the correct definition.

1. a male who takes part in a rodeo: _____
2. an event in which a person tries to stay on a male cow: _____
3. a building for keeping animals and their food: _____
4. a female who takes part in a rodeo: _____
5. an event in which a person rides a horse around large, round objects in a race: _____

bull riding

barrel racing

cowgirl

barn

cowboy

At the Rodeo

chuckwagon

tent

stove

At Stampede Park in Calgary, Canada, everyone is very busy. Some people are rushing from place to place, while others slowly work their way across the huge park carrying heavy loads. Some are cleaning, some are organizing, and others are setting up small shops, but they all have one thing in common: they have plenty of things to do! Then there are also the animals to consider. All kinds of creatures from sheep to horses are invading the park. And with them come the most important guests of all: the men and women who are coming to compete.

So what's all the excitement about? Everyone is getting ready for the start of one of the world's biggest outdoor rodeos: the famous **Calgary Stampede**.[1] The rodeo, or 'Stampede' as it's sometimes called, has been held in the city of Calgary in western Canada every year since 1912. This rodeo is special; it's unlike any other rodeo event of its kind.

---

[1] **Calgary Stampede:** the name of a special rodeo event in Calgary

CD 2, Track 03

As people and animals rush around Stampede Park, an older man wearing a large cowboy hat slowly walks through the crowd. As he does, he stops to say hello to people along the way, "Have a good afternoon, Wade," he says to one man, "Thank you for everything." He then approaches another nearby man, "Hi, Bob!" "Hi, Winston," the man replies with a smile and the two stop to have a short conversation.

Winston Bruce is the rodeo manager, or 'rodeo boss,' for the event, and he knows the people and the Stampede very well. He takes time from his busy day to explain just how big the rodeo is: "We have over 500 cowboys and cowgirls in 12 events here [at] Stampede Park throughout the ten days of rodeo." But the rodeo boss is not the only one preparing for the event. In different parts of Canada, competitors are getting ready for the Stampede, too. They have a lot do to as well—and a lot to be excited about!

At his home north of Calgary, Jason Glass is preparing to go to the Stampede. As he loads his horses into the horse **trailer**,[2] he jokes, "This is their last day of freedom." Jason and his horses are going to Calgary to compete in one of the biggest and most popular events at the rodeo: the chuckwagon races. As he continues to prepare for the trip, Jason talks about how important the Calgary Stampede is for him. "We train all year long to get these horses how we want them. It's our lives. It's definitely my life," he says. He then continues, "The whole year is focused on these ten days, so this is what it's all about."

Jason is only 33, but he has already been the **world champion**[3] of chuckwagon racing. And he's not the first one in his family to race; both Glass's father and grandfather were chuckwagon racers. "I'm a fourth-generation chuckwagon driver, you know. It started off back with my great grandfather, I guess, Tom Lauder. He started racing in 1923; he was in the first chuckwagon race at the Calgary Stampede. He raced then, and then my grandfather, Ronnie Glass, and my father, Tom Glass, and now myself. So we've been racing for some 75 years." He then explains why he does it, "I'm kind of an **adrenaline junkie**.[4] I love the excitement of it, the adventure, the thrill, the speed." But for Jason, it's not only about the excitement, "The biggest thing to me is the horses, you know. If it wasn't for the horses, I wouldn't be doing it."

---

[2]**trailer:** a vehicle on wheels pulled by another vehicle
[3]**world champion:** the best in the world
[4]**adrenaline junkie:** (slang) a person who enjoys the excitement of extreme and sometimes dangerous sports

Jason travels south through Canada's beautiful green open countryside to Calgary. Calgary is a busy, modern city in the province of Alberta, but once a year it goes 'cowboy crazy' for the Stampede. Once he arrives at Stampede Park, Jason takes the time to unload his horses and get them settled into the barn. It's not something that is easy to do with so many other strange horses around. The animals are a little nervous, but Jason keeps them under control.

As Jason takes care of his animals, the other competitors are settling in as well. Even though Jason has 15 years of racing experience, this year he's going to have some strong competition. One of his competitors is chuckwagon racer Kelly Sutherland. Kelly began chuckwagon racing more than 30 years ago. He's now 52 years old, and he's an eight-time world champion. He has also won the Calgary Stampede eight times. Kelly says, "I think the sport is very **unique**[5] and extremely dangerous. As far as for competitors, I think it's kind of like bull riding. It's not a matter of 'if' you're going to get hurt, it's a matter of 'when' and 'how bad.' That's the way I view it … if you stay in it as long as I have."

---

[5]**unique:** very different from other things; the only one of its kind

Fact Check: True or false?

1. The Calgary Stampede started in 1912.

2. There are over 500 events at the Stampede.

3. Jason comes from a family of chuckwagon racers.

4. Kelly has been racing for 15 years.

Kelly and Jason will be competing against 34 other chuckwagon racers, and in this competition, everyone wants to be the winner. They want to take home the $50,000 prize! But before anyone can compete, their wagons have to pass an official **inspection**.[6]

As Jason takes his chuckwagon in for inspection, he explains how the process works. "Every wagon is the same as far as length and width and size," he says. He then enters the inspection area and the workers quickly measure and weigh his wagon. As they begin calling out the measurements, Jason explains that his wagon can be heavier than the required weight, but not less than it. "It can't be any less, it can be more," he says as he waits to hear the results of the inspection. Suddenly he hears, "Gosh! 1,392!" The weight requirement for the race is 1,325 **pounds**[7] with the driver and his equipment. Jason's wagon is 67 pounds heavier than it needs to be! Jason is concerned, but the inspector tells him not to worry. They let the wagon settle on the scale for a while and Jason's wagon passes the inspection.

Jason's not the only one with weight problems. Kelly's chuckwagon weighs in about 20 pounds heavier than it should. Kelly plans to make a few changes before the race. For these racers, every little bit makes a difference!

---

[6]**inspection:** a close, careful look; examination
[7]**pound:** 1 pound = .45 kilograms

Jason and his team feed his horses before the race. His team also includes his 76-year-old grandmother, Iris. Iris has been coming to rodeos for most of her life and she loves them. As she helps the team hang Jason's sign on the side of the barn, she explains her feelings. "Oh, this is wonderful," she says. "It's all like a big, big family and we all [say], 'good morning,' and [if] somebody wants to borrow something, they run from barn to barn. It's just like a big family—here at the barn." However she then adds with a laugh, "But when they go over there to that **racetrack**[8] with their wagons, nobody's their friend! They're going to **outrun**[9] them!"

---

[8]**racetrack:** the place where a race happens
[9]**outrun:** go faster than someone or something else

It's the first night of the chuckwagon races and everyone is very excited. As the various teams bring their chuckwagons out onto the field, the announcer tells the crowd about the safety rules. Joe Carbury has been a racetrack announcer for 40 years and he knows the rules better than most. The chuckwagon race is divided into nine **heats**,[10] he explains, with four chuckwagons racing at a time. Each wagon is pulled by four horses.

In theory, chuckwagon racing models the 'old-time' cowboy lifestyle when they were out in the countryside caring for their cattle. Long ago, cowboy cooks often had to prepare meals for several groups of hungry cowboys in a short period of time. To do this, they had to be able to pack up their equipment and move to the next group as quickly as possible. Some believe that it eventually became a competition to see who could do this the fastest. Today's chuckwagon races are supposed to mirror this competition. In it, racers must pick up a heavy 'stove' (actually a barrel) and pack up their 'tent' (actually a cloth on the back of the wagon) before they race off.

---

[10]**heat:** an initial race to decide who will be in the final race

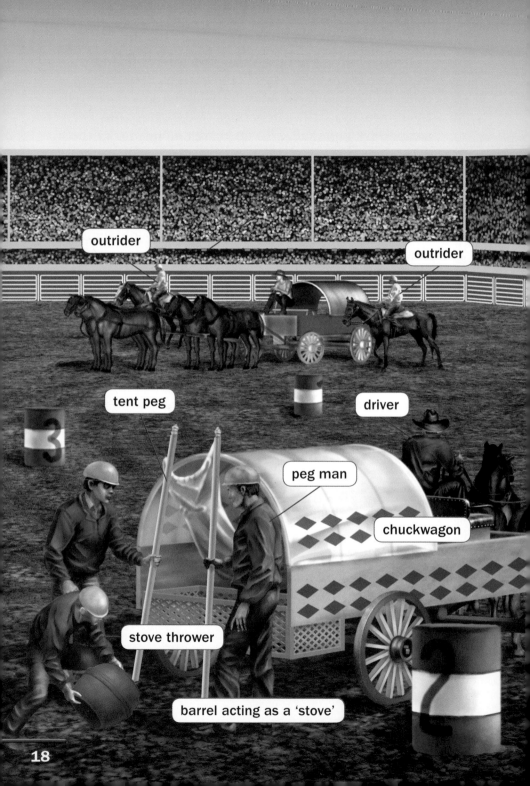

outrider

outrider

tent peg

driver

peg man

chuckwagon

stove thrower

barrel acting as a 'stove'

Before each heat, the chuckwagon drivers go to the center of the racetrack and the teams are lined up next to a series of barrels that have been set on the field. These are the starting positions for the race. They are assisted by four other men on horses, called 'outriders.' After they are on the field, one outrider stays in front of the wagon. His job is to hold the horses still. The other three outriders go behind the wagon.

These outriders are said to have been given the most dangerous duties. Carbury explains the responsibilities of these men. "One of them is referred to as the 'stove thrower,' and that's his job." The main responsibility of this man is to throw the stove into the wagon before it takes off. "Two other outriders behind the wagon," continues Carbury, "they're called the 'peg men.' They throw the tent pegs in the back of the wagon after the wagon starts moving—and believe me, it's moving!" After that, each wagon and all four outriders must race in a figure eight around a set of barrels. Then, all of the wagons and their outriders must race around the entire track and the first group to cross the finish line wins.

outrider

After nine exciting days, both Jason and Kelly are in the final chuckwagon race. This is the biggest race of the event. The chuckwagon driver who has the fastest time wins $50,000! Both racers excitedly prepare for the event. Kelly works with his team to be sure his chuckwagon is in the best condition possible. Huge crowds of people have gathered in Stampede Park and cheer noisily as they wait for the race to start. Back at the barn, Jason and his team carefully check their horses to be sure they are ready. Out near the racetrack, the outriders put on their protective equipment as they get ready for the race, as well. Who will be the final winner? Nobody knows, but one competitor knows what he needs to win …

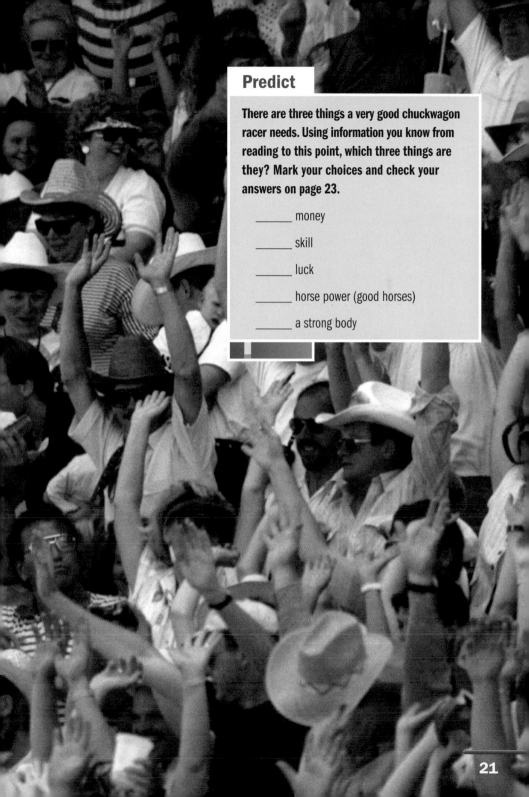

Predict

There are three things a very good chuckwagon racer needs. Using information you know from reading to this point, which three things are they? Mark your choices and check your answers on page 23.

_____ money

_____ skill

_____ luck

_____ horse power (good horses)

_____ a strong body

According to Kelly, a champion really needs three things. He explains in his own words, "I think there [are] three key things that make a chuckwagon driver a champion," he says. "The first one is horse power, and that's 50 percent of the equation. The second most important thing—and I'd say it's 25 percent of the equation—is skill. And the last and most important thing that's got to follow you is … 25 percent of it's luck. I mean, it's **lady luck**.[11] And if she's not riding with you—I don't care how good you are. You're out. You're done. **You're toast**."[12]

---

[11] **lady luck:** *(slang)* good luck
[12] **you're toast:** *(slang)* an expression meaning 'you're finished' or 'you lose'

Everyone is finally ready at the racetrack and the crowds can hardly wait. Jason's grandmother is begging for the race to begin as she waits to cheer Jason on. "Okay, blow the **horn**,"[13] she says impatiently, "Hurry up!" Then suddenly, a horn blows loudly and the race begins! The stove throwers quickly get their barrels, or 'stoves,' into the backs of the wagons as the peg men pull up the pegs and put them in the back, too. The outriders then run quickly to their horses to get out onto the racetrack. It's incredibly exciting as the four chuckwagons and their outriders race around the barrels before speeding onto the track.

Kelly gets to the front of the racing pack and leads the race until the final turn on the track. Then, amazingly, Jason Glass suddenly pulls up closer from the rest of the racers—and he does it very fast! He gets closer and closer … and closer! Suddenly the announcer's voice breaks through the cheering crowd, "Look at the finish! Jason Glass is **closing in**![14] Kelly's trying to hold on! But it's Jason Glass!" As the other teams cross the finish line, Jason seems to have won the race! However, in chuckwagon racing almost anything can happen— and this time it's something unexpected …

---

[13]**horn:** a piece of equipment that gives a loud warning sound
[14]**close in:** approach; get closer

Unfortunately, one of Jason's outriders was late crossing the finish line. Jason has to add one second to his time. Although it's a very small amount, it's enough to cost Jason the race. Kelly's time is now faster. Tonight lady luck is shining on Kelly—he's the winner! Later, after the race, Kelly talks about what it feels like to be the champion chuckwagon racer. "Unbelievable," he says. "It feels so good to win, you know? [It] feels so bad to lose, and so good to win. That's just life, eh?"

Back in one of the other barns, Jason has his own opinion about luck. "You know, luck comes with hard work," he says. "I plan on getting stronger every year. I'm not going to slow down. I'm not going to weaken—you can't in this sport! As soon as you take a breath, someone else gets better. So you [have] got to keep carrying on." Jason knows that he has to keep working hard and getting stronger to win, and that's what makes a real chuckwagon racing champion!

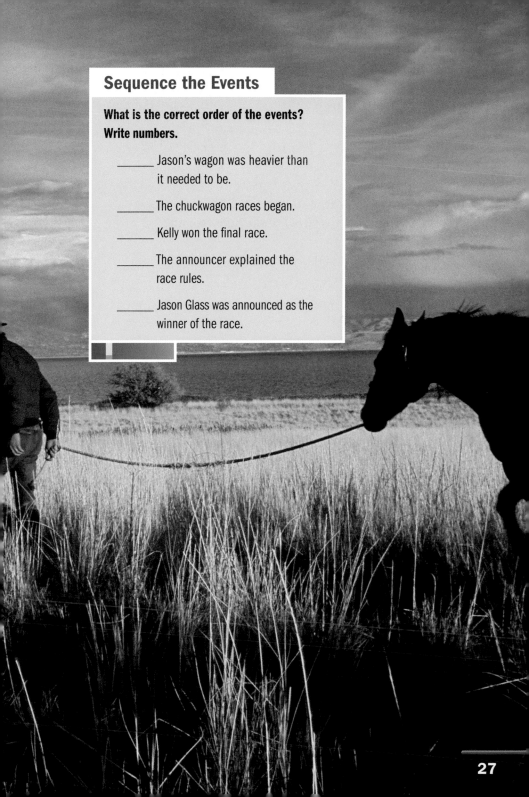

Sequence the Events

What is the correct order of the events? Write numbers.

_____ Jason's wagon was heavier than it needed to be.

_____ The chuckwagon races began.

_____ Kelly won the final race.

_____ The announcer explained the race rules.

_____ Jason Glass was announced as the winner of the race.

After You Read

1. The Calgary Stampede is _____ other rodeo events.
    A. close to
    B. the same as
    C. different from
    D. exactly like

2. In paragraph 2 on page 7, to whom does 'we' refer?
    A. cowboys and cowgirls
    B. rodeo organizers
    C. chuckwagon racers
    D. Stampede horses

3. Jason Glass feels that chuckwagon racing is each of the following EXCEPT:
    A. an easy event to train for
    B. part of his family history
    C. important in his life
    D. the focus of his year

4. How many generations of the Glass family have been chuckwagon racers?
    A. one
    B. two
    C. three
    D. four

5. In paragraph 2 on page 10, 'extremely' can be replaced by:
    A. a little
    B. sometimes
    C. not
    D. very

6. What happens when Jason's wagon is inspected?
    A. He isn't allowed to compete.
    B. He passes the test easily.
    C. He has some small problems, but passes.
    D. His chuckwagon is too light.

7. An appropriate heading for page 14 is:
   A. Barn Friends Are Racetrack Friends
   B. Grandmother Glass Loves the Rodeo
   C. Iris and Jason Ride Together
   D. Grandmother's First Race

8. Which of the following does NOT describe what outriders do?
   A. They race with the chuckwagon.
   B. They throw tent pegs.
   C. They hold the horses steady.
   D. They all stay in front of the wagon.

9. What do the teams do to prepare for the final race?
   A. check their chuckwagon's condition
   B. check their horses
   C. put on their safety equipment
   D. all of the above

10. On page 23, to what 'she' is Kelly referring?
   A. a horse
   B. lady luck
   C. a wagon driver
   D. an outrider

11. Why did Kelly become the champion?
   A. Kelly's outrider made a mistake.
   B. Jason closed in suddenly.
   C. Kelly had bad luck.
   D. none of the above

12. On page 26, what does the writer think makes a real chuckwagon champion?
   A. hard work and practice
   B. horsepower and skill
   C. lady luck and good outriders
   D. quick speed and family history

The Changing of RODEO

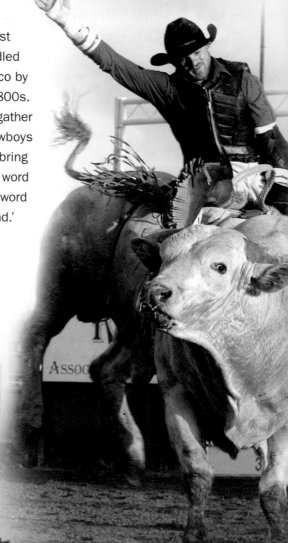

T oday's rodeos are very different from the original cowboy gatherings. The first cowboys were workers who handled cattle that were brought to Mexico by the Spanish in the 1700s and 1800s. Once a year, the workers had to gather all their cattle. The job of the cowboys was to surround the cattle and bring them together in one place. The word 'rodeo' comes from the Spanish word '*rodear*' which means 'to surround.' When the work was done, the cowboys often tested the skills they used in some of the daily activities in what is now called a rodeo.

In bull riding, it's not a question of 'if' you'll get hurt, but 'when'!

In the 1800s, the raising of cattle became an important industry in the western United States. Soon, the cowboy way of life spread to the American West and the popularity of the rodeo grew with it. However, by the mid-1800s, railroads began to take over the job of moving cattle from place to place. It became harder for cowboys to earn a living, so some cowboys started making money by holding contests. These gatherings eventually grew into well-organized shows that people paid to watch.

Slowly, the types of events at rodeos became more varied. For example, the dangerous sport of bull riding was introduced. Bull riders say that it isn't a question of if they are going to get hurt, but when they are going to get hurt. In this event, a cowboy wraps a rope around a bull's body. He then holds on to the rope with one hand and is not allowed to touch his body or the bull's with the other hand. The goal is to stay on the bull for at least eight seconds. If he is thrown off, rodeo helpers get the bull's attention so the cowboy can run to safety.

At one time, cowgirls competed against men in rodeos. People liked seeing men and women challenge each other in these contests of strength and skill. However, in the 1940s, women's events were dropped in order to allow men to earn more money at rodeos. Nowadays though, there are rodeos that feature events for both women and men, as well as children.

> "These gatherings eventually grew into well-organized shows that people paid to watch."

CD 2, Track 04

Word Count: 349
Time: _____

Vocabulary List

adrenaline junkie (8)
barn (3, 10, 14, 20, 26)
barrel (racing) (3, 17, 19, 24)
bull riding (3, 10)
cattle (2, 17)
chuckwagon (2, 3, 8, 10, 11, 13, 17, 18, 19, 20, 21, 23, 24, 26, 27)
close in (24)
cowboy (2, 3, 7, 10, 17)
cowgirl (2, 3, 7)
heat (17, 19)
horn (24)
inspection (13)
lady luck (23, 26)
outrun (14)
pound (13)
racetrack (14, 17, 19, 20, 24)
rodeo (2, 3, 4, 7, 14)
stove (2, 3, 17, 18, 19, 24)
tent (2, 3, 17, 18, 19)
trailer (8)
unique (10)
world champion (8, 10)
you're toast (23)